Sort It Out!
Stories with Different Issues

Teacher's Book

by Julie Garnett and Julia Timlin
Pupil's anthology by Jan Mark

Contents

Section 1: for Below Average Readers

Guided reading and writing lessons using: The New Boy

Teaching Notes for Guided Reading	2
Teaching Notes for Guided Writing	3
Copymaster 1: explaining the issues	4
Copymaster 2: letter writing frame – explaining a problem	5

Guided reading and writing lessons using: The Secret Maze

Teaching Notes for Guided Reading	6
Teaching Notes for Guided Writing	7
Copymaster 3: writing critically about an issue	8
Copymaster 4: diary writing about being bullied	9

Section 2: for Average Readers

Guided reading and writing lessons using: Past and Present

Teaching Notes for Guided Reading	10
Teaching Notes for Guided Writing	11
Copymaster 5: writing an alternative ending	12
Copymaster 6: changing sentences, e.g. positive to negative	13

Guided reading and writing lessons using: Louie and Glenda

Teaching Notes for Guided Reading	14
Teaching Notes for Guided Writing	15
Copymaster 7: sorting true/false statements	16
Copymaster 8: writing character sketches	17

Section 3: for Above Average Readers

Guided reading and writing lessons using: The Game

Teaching Notes for Guided Reading	18
Teaching Notes for Guided Writing	19
Copymaster 9: 'difficult words' cards	20
Copymaster 10: writing frame – a letter of support	21

Guided reading and writing lessons using: Never Go With Strangers

Teaching Notes for Guided Reading	22
Teaching Notes for Guided Writing	23
Copymaster 11: questions on the text	24
Copymaster 12: story planner	25

Longman

Edinburgh Gate
Harlow, Essex

Sort It Out!
Stories with Different Issues

Year 4 Term 3

Section **1** Below Average Level

The New Boy

Guided Reading

Key Objectives

- Identify social, moral or cultural issues in stories, e.g. the dilemmas faced by characters or the moral of the story.
- Discuss how the characters deal with these issues.
- Locate evidence in the text.

This extract can be studied over two guided reading sessions.

Introduction 1

- Introduce the extract by a general discussion. *What did you feel like when you first started school/started in this class?*
- Explain that the text is about a boy called William who is a 'new' boy joining the class.
- Tell the group the names of the characters, including the cat (e.g. put them on cards and read them together).
- Identify any other difficult vocabulary and clarify the meaning.

Reading and Discussion 1

- Ask the children to read aloud quietly up to '… empty space at their table?'
- Support individual children by suggesting appropriate reading strategies.

Returning to the Text for Evaluation and Analysis 1

- Discuss the story so *far. Why do you think the cat is so important?* Encourage the children to look at how the cat provides the link between the characters *(Do all the characters like the cat? How do you know?)*
- What does William do and why is it a problem? Ask the children to predict what is going to happen next.

Introduction 2

- Briefly recap on the story so far, mentioning the characters' names and identifying what William had done to Jane by finding the evidence in the text.

Reading and Discussion 2

- Ask the children to read in pairs. Support pairs with appropriate reading strategies where necessary.
- Ask for their initial responses to the story. *Is William being horrible to Jane? Why? Why do you think the other boys are taking William's side?*

Returning to the Text for Evaluation and Analysis 2

- Take each main character and discuss the dilemma from their perspective.
- Ask the pairs to discuss one way in which the characters might try to sort out the problem.
- Share ideas and try to come to a mutual agreement about how the problem might be solved.

© Pearson Education Limited 2000

Sort It Out!
Stories with Different Issues

Year 4 Term 3

Section ❶ Below Average Level

The New Boy

Guided Writing

Key Objectives

- Write critically about an issue or dilemma raised in a story, explaining the problem.
- Give a course of action to resolve the problem.

Task

Explain the dilemma for Jane and suggest a course of action she could take to resolve the situation.

Each child needs a copy of the guided reading book and Copymaster ❶.

Introduction

- Ask the children to retell the main points of the extract from *Taking the Cat's Way Home*.
- Introduce the task and distribute **Copymaster ❶**.
- Discuss the purpose for the writing, e.g. a class book on 'suggested ways to sort out problems'. *Refer back to your guided reading books if you need to.* Leave the characters' name cards in the middle of the table.

Children Writing Individually

- Support each individual as necessary with spelling strategies, especially phonic segmentation and blending. Refer to guided reading books and name cards where appropriate.
- Stop the children at certain points to share ideas, discuss and clarify aspects of the task and their writing.

Evaluation

- Ask the children to read their explanations of the issue in the story to each other. *Do we agree?* Ask for comments and suggestions for improvement.
- Share ideas about what Jane could do to resolve the dilemma and compare.

- Identify successes and difficulties evident during the session.
- Summarise what the children have been doing.

Suggested Independent Activities

- William was new at school. Write what happened from his point of view.
- What could Mr. Singh do to sort out the problem? Record your ideas.
- You are Jane. Write a letter to your teacher explaining what William did to make you feel so unhappy. Use **Copymaster ❷**.
- You are Furlong. Explain your journey to school in the mornings. Who do you see and what do they say and do?

© Pearson Education Limited 2000

Sort It Out!
Stories with Different Issues

Copymaster 1

The New Boy

A Problem for Jane

When Jane was walking to school with _____
_____
_____
_____
_____
_____.

Mr Singh introduced William to the class and sat opposite Jane, but
_____
_____
_____
_____
_____
_____.

Jane needs to sort out the problem. I think Jane needs to _____
_____
_____
_____
_____
_____
_____.

© Pearson Education Limited 2000

Letter To Mr Singh

Dear Mr Singh,

   I have a problem and need your help. I was walking to school with Andrea when _____
_____
_____
_____.

   When William sat on our table _____
_____
_____
_____.

   At break time William, Habib and Matthew _____
_____
_____
_____.

   After break, Matthew and Habib were horrible to me, they
_____
_____
_____.

   Can you help me to sort it out?

            From _____

Sort It Out! Stories with Different Issues — Year 4 Term 3 — Section 1 Below Average Level

The Secret Maze

Guided Reading

Key Objectives
- Identify social, moral or cultural issues in stories, e.g. the dilemmas faced by characters or the moral of the story.
- Discuss how the characters deal with them.
- Locate evidence in the text.

This extract can be studied over two guided reading sessions.

Introduction 1
- Set the context for the reading by asking *What is a bully?* Discuss any personal experiences of the group.
- Explain that the text is about a boy called Joe who has a key to a secret maze. (Clarify the meaning of 'maze' if necessary.) He told another boy (Akash) about it, but Akash couldn't see the maze.
- Find the names of the characters in the text and read them together.
- Identify any other difficult vocabulary and clarify their meaning.

Reading and Discussion 1
- Read the first four sentences to the group. *As you read, imagine what it must be like to be Joe.*
- Ask the children to read quietly up to 'It was his secret' at the end of the chapter.
- Support individual children by suggesting appropriate reading strategies.

Returning to the Text for Evaluation and Analysis 1
- Suggest that the children look back at the text. *It says that neither Akash or Tim were bullies. Do you agree? Why are they so horrible to Joe?*
- *Is there really a maze? Why can Joe see it and the others can't? Why do you think the book is called 'The Snow Maze'?* Ask the children to predict what is going to happen next.

Introduction 2
Briefly recap on the story so far.

Reading and Discussion 2
- Read the first four sentences to the group as an introduction to the reading.
- Ask the children to read the rest of the text in pairs. Support pairs with appropriate reading strategies where necessary.

Returning to the Text for Evaluation and Analysis 2
- *Why do you think the others continued to call Joe names? How would you describe Irrum?* Take each character and discuss their role in the story. Get the children to justify their answers.
- *Do you think Irrum will be able to see the maze? Why?*
- Share ideas about possible outcomes to the story. Try to solve the dilemma for Joe.

© Pearson Education Limited 2000

Sort It Out!
Stories with Different Issues

Year 4 Term 3

Section ❶ Below Average Level

The Secret Maze

Guided Writing

Key Objectives

- Write critically about an issue or dilemma raised in a story, explaining the problem.
- Give a course of action to resolve the problem.

Task

Record your feelings about how Joe was treated in the extract. Suggest a course of action he and Irrum could take to resolve the situation.

Each child needs a copy of the guided reading book and Copymaster ❸.

Introduction

- Recall the main points of the extract from *The Snow Maze*. Set the task and look through and discuss **Copymaster ❸**.
- Discuss the purpose for the writing, e.g. adding to a class book on 'suggested ways to sort out problems'.
- Brainstorm a list of useful words and chart on the board. *Refer back to your guided reading books to help you remember the sequence of events in the story.*

Children Writing Individually

- Support each individual as necessary with appropriate spelling strategies.
- Refer to the useful words board and add more if necessary.
- Stop the children at certain points to share ideas, discuss and clarify aspects of the task and their writing.

Evaluation

- Ask the children to share their work with the whole group. Make comparisons between different opinions.
- *How can the two characters make the situation better for Joe?* Read out ideas and discuss suggestions.
- Identify successes and difficulties that were evident during the session.
- Summarise what the children have been doing and ask for their comments about the task.

Suggested Independent Activities

- Write a story about a bullying incident.
- Write the story as if you were Akash. Why did Joe upset you?
- Draw Joe's maze.
- You are Joe. Write a diary entry about being bullied at school. Describe what happened and how you feel. Use **Copymaster ❹**.

© Pearson Education Limited 2000

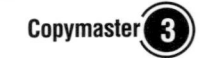

The Secret Maze

I think Joe is _____
_____
_____
_____.

It made me feel _____ when I read about the way he was treated by the other boys, especially when they _____
_____
_____.

I can't understand why _____
_____
_____
_____.

I think Joe and Irrum should _____
_____
_____
_____.

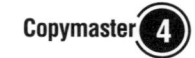

Joe's Diary Entry

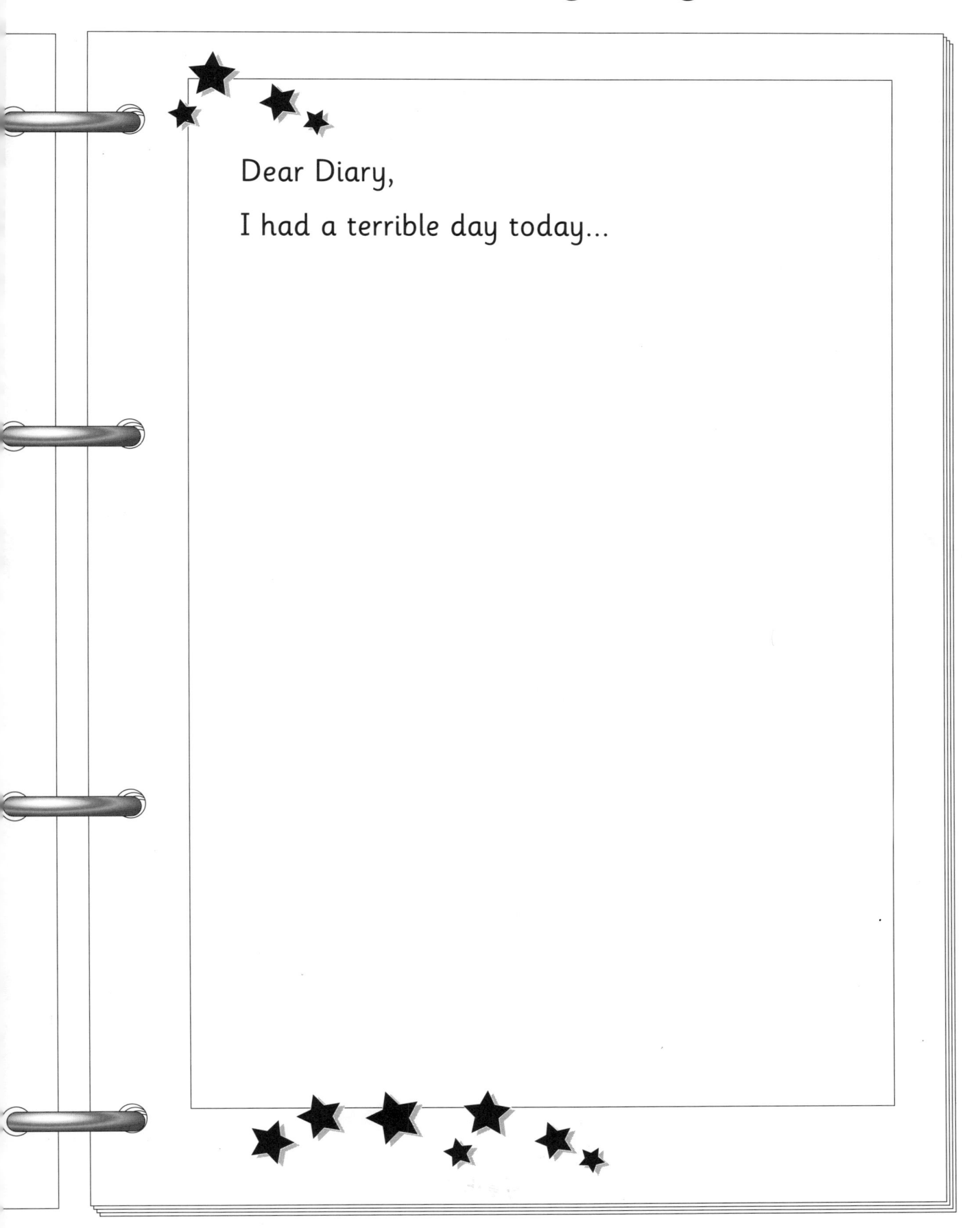

Dear Diary,

I had a terrible day today…

Sort It Out!
Stories with Different Issues

Year 4 Term 3

Section ❷ Average Level

Past and Present

Guided Reading

Key Objectives

- Identify social, moral or cultural issues in stories, e.g. the dilemmas faced by characters or the moral of the story.
- Discuss how the characters deal with them.
- Locate evidence in the text.

Introduction

- Start with a general discussion about Grandparents and Great Grandparents. Discuss things the children notice they say and do.
- Introduce the text, telling the children that it comes from a book called 'All the Kings and Queens'. *Why do you think the book is called* All the Kings and Queens? *Discuss the possibilities then read the first section, to the group, up to '... row of them. I remember.'* Now why do you think the book might be called All the Kings and Queens? *Relate back to the initial discussion.*

Reading and Discussion

- Ask the children to read up to 'there were no kings and queens'. *As you read, think about why each character seems annoyed or frustrated.* Allow children to offer ideas, referring back to the text for evidence.
- *What is happening to Great Grandma?* Children read the next section to find answer. Discuss Gran's comments.
- *Who is Great Gran confusing Ken with?* Ask the group how they would handle a situation like this. They may have some real experiences to share. Compare how Great Grandma is feeling with the feelings of Ken and Gran.
- *Kenny tries to help his great grandma. What does he do?* Draw out how he stops trying to convince her that there were no kings and queens and tries to 'play along' with her. *Why does he change and 'play along' with her instead?*

Returning to the Text for Evaluation and Analysis

- *What is the problem or dilemma for Ken?* Lead the children into identifying that older people often start to relive their memories.
- *What does 'the house was suddenly full of ghosts' mean?*
- Ask the children whether they feel this is an easy or difficult situation to deal with.

© Pearson Education Limited 2000

Sort It Out!
Stories with Different Issues   Year 4 Term 3   Section ❷ Average Level

Past and Present

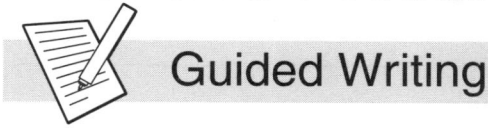

Guided Writing

Key Objectives
- Write an alternative ending for a known story.
- Discuss how this would change the reader's view of the characters and events of the original story.

Task
Imagine that when the *Courier* was published the photograph *did* show Ken with all the kings and queens of Europe. Write the changed ending to the extract.

The children will each need a copy of **Copymaster ❺** and their guided reading books.

Introduction
- Recap on the original extract and discuss how Great Grandma was certain that Ken would 'have his picture in the paper with all the kings and queens'.
- This did not happen, *but imagine that it did!* Read the task and ask the children to write a different ending. Talk through some ideas with the group about how Ken might have met the kings and queens of Europe.

Children Writing Individually
- Give children a copy of **Copymaster ❺**.
- Support each child as necessary with appropriate spelling strategies and through differentiated questioning.

Evaluation
- Share each new ending with the group, and ask for suggestions for improvement and positive comments.
- Discuss how the change in the storyline changes the way the characters behave towards each other and it then causes another problem to resolve. *How do Great Gran, Gran and Ken feel and act now?*

Suggested Independent Activities
- Write a story about someone who is reliving the past.
- Change the sentences on **Copymaster ❻**.
- Prepare the extract 'Past and Present' as a short drama for a presentation to the whole class.

© Pearson Education Limited 2000

Sort It Out!
Stories with Different Issues

Copymaster 5

Past and Present

Changing a Story

When the *Courier* was published the photograph showed Ken with all the kings and queens of Europe.

© Pearson Education Limited 2000

12

Changing Sentences

Either:
- Make a statement into a question or a question into a statement.
- Make a positive statement into a negative or a negative into a positive.
- Make a past tense sentence into a present and a present into a past.

Statement: There was a row of kings and queens.

Question:

Positive statement: Ken was there with all the other people.

Negative statement:

Past tense: The house was full of ghosts.

Present tense:

Question: Shall I show Great Grandma?

Statement:

Past tense: The *Courier* is published on Tuesdays.

Present tense:

Past tense: There were not any kings and queens.

Present tense:

What did you have to do to each of the sentences?

Sort It Out!
Stories with Different Issues

Year 4 Term 3

Section ❷ Average Level

Louie and Glenda

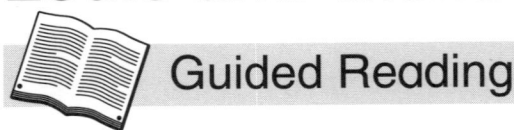

Guided Reading

Key Objectives
- Identify social, moral or cultural issues in stories, e.g. the dilemmas faced by characters or the moral of the story.
- Discuss how the characters deal with these issues.
- Locate evidence in the text.

Use **Copymaster ❼**, cut up and stuck on individual cards for sorting.

Introduction
- *There is a problem in the story today involving friendship. What do you consider to be the qualities of a good friend? What do you expect from your friends?* Chart the children's responses.
- Talk about the different levels of friendship – home, school, close, casual, just to talk to, etc.
- Introduce the extract, and ask the children to skim over the text and identify any difficult words. Discuss and clarify the meaning.

Reading and Discussion
- *Think about how you would feel if you were Louie.*
- Children read the text quietly to themselves. Support by commenting on intonation and expression as you listen to each child in turn. Suggest appropriate strategies for reading when necessary.

Returning to the Text for Evaluation and Analysis
- Discuss the children's feelings about the text. *Describe your feelings if you were Louie.* Refer back to the brainstorm about friendship and compare. *Is Glenda a true friend? Why/why not?*
- Use **Copymaster ❼** and sort the statements into true or false, referring to the text for evidence. Discuss each statement. The children may have different views about some of the cards and will need to come to a group agreement.
- Finally, ask the group to think about how lonely Louie must feel. *Do you have any suggestions to help her mix in more with her classmates?*

© Pearson Education Limited 2000

Sort It Out!
Stories with Different Issues — Year 4 Term 3 — Section 2 Average Level

Louie and Glenda
Guided Writing

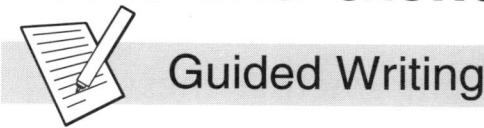

Key Objective
- Write character sketches focusing on small details (Year 4 Term 1).

Task
Write character sketches of Louie and Glenda.

Each child will need their guided reading book and a copy of Copymaster 8.

Introduction
- Ask the group to retell the main points of the extract. *What is the problem facing the main character?* Chart the issues as they are raised. *Why are they a problem for Louie and not for Glenda?*
- Start to draw comparisons between the two characters. Write these on the board.
- Explain the task and give each child a copy of **Copymaster 8**. Generate the first few ideas together before the children attempt the writing on their own.

Children Writing Individually
- Keep the ideas visible on the board and refer to them when necessary.
- Help individuals through discussion, looking back at the text for evidence.
- Support each child, as necessary, with ideas and spelling strategies.

Evaluation
- Focus on each character in turn. Share observations and how the point of view was arrived at. Encourage children to question and debate points made.
- Discuss difficulties and successes evident during the session.
- Children might like to work with a partner to complete the task.

Suggested Independent Activities
- Write a story about a child who is lonely and wants some friends.
- Using **Copymaster 7** as a model, make a true or false game about another story.
- Use **Copymaster 8** to write appropriate adjectives to describe each character.
- Write a happy ending for 'Louie and Glenda'.

© Pearson Education Limited 2000

Sort It Out!
Stories with Different Issues

Copymaster 7

Louie and Glenda

True or False

After reading this extract, use the text to find out whether these statements are true or false.

Work as a group and discuss your decisions.

True	False

Glenda is a good friend to Louie.

Louie is a confident girl.

Glenda and Louie are in the choir.

Joanne Smith talked to Glenda.

Louie was in Mrs Thomas' class.

Louie was moving house.

Louie wanted to be friends with Wayne.

Louie makes friends easily.

Glenda and Louie are best friends.

© Pearson Education Limited 2000

Sort It Out!
Stories with Different Issues

Copymaster 8

Louie and Glenda

Character Sketches

Glenda

Louie

© Pearson Education Limited 2000

Sort It Out! | Year 4 Term 3 | Section ❸ Above Average Level
Stories with Different Issues

The Game

Guided Reading

Key Objectives

- Identify social, moral or cultural issues in stories, e.g. the dilemmas faced by characters or the moral of the story.
- Discuss how the characters deal with these issues.
- Locate evidence in the text.

You will need a copy of Copymaster ❾ – cut up and mounted on separate cards.

Introduction

- *The dilemma for the character (David) in this extract is how to handle his younger brother who displays some difficult behaviour.* The reading will benefit from a group discussion about brothers and sisters and getting blamed 'when it's not my fault'!
- Spread the 'difficult word' cards from Copymaster ❾ on the table and discuss to clarify the meaning. Find the relevant sentences in the text if necessary. [Flak = anti-aircraft fire]

Reading and Discussion

- Ask the children to read the first paragraph to themselves. *What can you find out from this introduction?*
- Decide on a 'who's who', like a cast list, possibly list on the board. *How old do you think Peter is? Describe the scene.*
- Ask them to continue reading the next seven paragraphs down to 'Don't be such a bully.' Encourage the children to share their views about David and Peter and the relationship they have. *Is David being unfairly treated by his Mum or is Peter being unfairly treated by his brother?* Extend their answers by asking *Why do you think that? How do you know?*
- Ask the group to continue reading to the end.

Returning to the Text for Evaluation and Analysis

- *Do you still feel the same about the characters after reading the rest of the text?* The group may have differing views, but need to support their argument with evidence.
- Encourage the children to identify the issue for David ('He always chases the foreign ones', 'He was a dirty foreign spy.' 'Peter growled'). *Do you think Peter is being racist or do you think David is overreacting?*
- *Could David manage the situation in a different way?*
- *Do you think that owning and playing with toy guns and knives encourages children to be violent? What are the arguments for and against?*

© Pearson Education Limited 2000

Sort It Out!
Stories with Different Issues

Year 4 Term 3

Section ❸ Above Average Level

The Game

Guided Writing

Key Objectives
- Write critically about a character's dilemma in a story.
- Offer alternative courses of action.

Task
You are a friend of Peter's. Draft a letter to him expressing your support and offering him some different ways of dealing with his younger brother.

Each child will need a copy of Copymaster ❿ and their guided reading book.

Introduction
- Recap on the dilemma faced by David. Explain the task.
- Give out copies of Copymaster ❿ and go through it with the group. Remind them this is a draft and they will have the opportunity of redrafting with a partner towards the end of the session.
- Ask the children to offer some suggestions for coping with Peter. Chart ideas.

Children Writing Individually
- Using their own copy of Copymaster ❿, the children can start to draft their letters.
- Stop children at relevant points to share ideas or to make a teaching point.
- Support individuals by noting and discussing points as they draft them.
- Encourage them to extend their answers, by using a range of connectives in order to write more complex sentences.

Evaluation
- Ask each child to read their drafts. Encourage the rest of the group to ask questions and offer suggestions for improvement.
- Put the children into pairs and allow them time to redraft and edit their work together.
- Discuss difficulties and successes evident during the session.

Suggested Independent Activities
- You are one of the 'foreign' students that Peter has shot! Write to him and tell him how you feel about his silly behaviour.
- Find and record the dictionary definitions of the 'difficult words' on Copymaster ❾.
- Write a story about a problem between brothers and sisters and how they could resolve it.

© Pearson Education Limited 2000

Difficult Vocabulary

Cut out these words and mount them on cards to share with the group.

camouflaged flak helmet	
armoury	intercept
stashed away	
curious	interfering
persisted	grenades
automatically	
cantered	retrieved

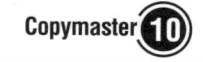

A Letter to David from a Friend

Dear David,

I am really sorry to hear you are having problems with Peter. Especially _____

_____

_____.

I'm sure the 'foreign' students _____

_____

_____.

When my younger brother was Peter's age he _____

_____

_____.

and I dealt with it by _____

_____

_____.

On the other hand, perhaps you could try _____

_____

_____.

I hope this is some help. See you soon,

_____

Sort It Out! Stories with Different Issues — Year 4 Term 3 — Section ❸ Above Average Level

Never Go With Strangers

Guided Reading

Key Objectives
- Identify social, moral or cultural issues in stories, e.g. the dilemmas faced by characters or the moral of the story.
- Discuss how the characters deal with these issues.
- Locate evidence in the text.

Introduction
- Introduce the extract with a general discussion. *How often do you go to town/go shopping? Who do you usually go with? Do or have you ever gone to town on your own?* Briefly explain that the text is about a girl called Sallie who may be in town and is trying to find a bus stop to travel somewhere else.
- Continue the discussion by asking *Do you get a lift or do you catch a bus? Have you ever missed a bus?*

Reading and Discussion
- *Read the first paragraph on your own and see if we can establish where Sallie is and what dilemma or problem she is facing.* Extend the children's basic answers by *'How do you know? Where does it give you that idea?'* Relate the first sentence to the last which gives the clue to the problem.
- Read the second and third paragraphs to the group. Discuss how the author has created a sense of urgency through the repetition of 'bus(es)' and 'stop(s)' and the use of words and phrases like 'calm down', 'in a panic she grabbed').
- Ask the children to read to the end on their own. *Do Sallie's problems remain the same or do they change?*

Returning to the Text for Evaluation and Analysis
- Through the group discussion, draw out Sallie's feelings and the building of her panic throughout the extract. Look at the use of *italics* and the use of speech.
- *How well does Sallie manage the situation?* Decide what is making her so worried.
- *What is the issue at the end?* Ask the group what they would do in that situation.

© Pearson Education Limited 2000

Sort It Out!
Stories with Different Issues — Year 4 Term 3 — Section ❸ Above Average Level

Never Go With Strangers

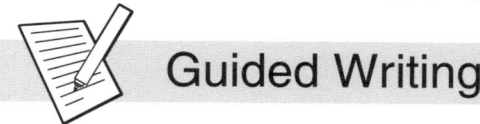

Guided Writing

Key Objective
- Explain the problems faced by the main character and give different courses of action.

Task
Complete **Copymaster ⓫**.

Each child will need: their guided reading book, a notebook or whiteboard and a copy of **Copymaster ⓫**.

Introduction

- Recap the extract and explain the task. Tell the group that they will be focusing on giving clear, full answers to the questions and will have the opportunity to redraft and edit each answer before they write it on the sheet.
- Go through the questions and remind the children that they discussed Sallie's dilemmas and issues during their guided reading session which should help them now. *You need to include evidence in your answers.*
- Do the first question together, scribing on the board. *Is that clear? Can we say that another way? Where is the evidence?* Add quotes if appropriate.

Children Writing Individually

- Address each question separately. Give the children the chance to refer back to the text for evidence to include in their answers.
- Children write initial responses on their whiteboards, supporting individual children through discussion and questioning.
- Discuss each answer and the variety of responses. Children can then redraft and edit if necessary before transferring to their **Copymaster ⓫**.

Evaluation

- *Are you clearer about answering a question fully? What new skill(s) have you learned from this session?* Identify using the text, redrafting and making sure the answers are clear.

Independent Follow-up

- The group may need an independent session to complete their work.

Suggested Independent Activities

- Write about 'missing my bus'.
- Read some of the other stories about issues in your guided reading book.
- Plan a story which has a dilemma for the main character. Use **Copymaster ⓬**.

© Pearson Education Limited 2000

Questions about the Text

Name: _____

How old do you think Sallie is? What clues are there?

Where do you think Sallie has been and where is she going?

How does the author manage to create the feeling of panic? Give some examples to illustrate your answer.

The author has decided to use three characters. Why?

What dilemma is Sallie facing? What is the issue raised at the end of the story?

Should Sallie go with the man or not? Give two suggestions and also write down what could happen if she does either.